More Precious Than Pearls
Written by Nora McElwain & Muna Haddad
Illustrated by Nora McElwain

Copyright © 2023. All rights reserved.
Published by Born Twice Books

ISBN 979-8-98880368-0-7

www.BornTwiceBooks.com

Dedicated to
Our Lord and Savior,
Jesus Christ,
Who takes
The grittiest grains of sand
And transforms them
Into pearls of great price

::: FOREWORD :::

There are many blessings that I have received from my Heavenly Father. My Salvation would be at the top of that list. The next would be my family.

The Bible speaks of the great responsibility we have been given to raise our children in the fear and admonition of The Lord. There is no greater joy than sharing The Gospel with your family. That is the first and most important role as a parent. The Bible tells us, "Train up a child in the way he should go…"

I am so glad that God led Nora McElwain and Muna Haddad to collaborate in the making of this fabulous masterpiece, "More Precious than Pearls." Finding a jewel like this book will help you as a parent to share the good news of Christ.

Each page is masterfully done with a biblical truth and scriptural reference, with your child in mind. The artwork will keep the attention of children of all ages, while teaching them truths from The Bible. It is a great addition to your daily Bible reading. Every single page is pointing the reader to their personal relationship and walk with Jesus Christ.

It is with great honor that I write the foreword for this book, and I look forward to the many lives that will be touched for years to come.

Gary W. Edwards
Pastor
Landmark Baptist Church
Easley, South Carolina

The question is, "Which do you believe?"
Words that bring Life, or words that deceive?

Do you believe the strange things people say?
And all those bad thoughts that lead you astray?

Or do you believe
you are made with a plan?
That God can give you victory
over the enemy of the land?

As soon as you realize
you are weak and feeble,
Seek help from the Lord,
for He is strong and able.

His Spirit will remove the scales from your eyes.
His Word will divide the truth from the lies.

Your heart will rejoice
when you know that you know,

No length is too far for His love to go.

Begin today to believe the truth:
God gave His only begotten Son to rescue you.

If you trust and believe
in the King of Kings,
He'll make you His child—
what joy that will bring!

You'll choose good thoughts and speak kind words,

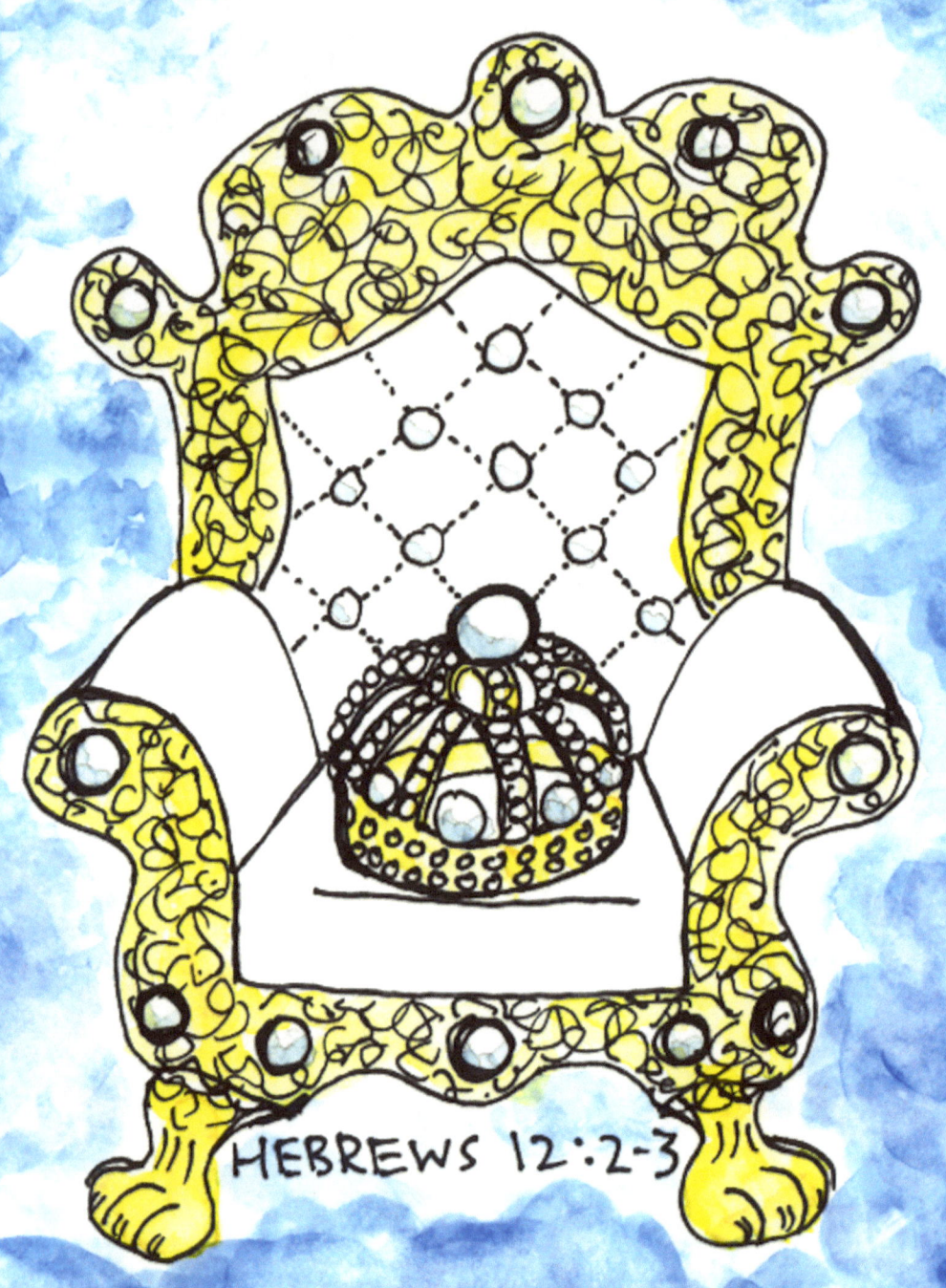

Encourage yourself—
you are loved beyond measure.
Jesus came just for you,
for you are His treasure!

 # PEARLS OF WISDOM

Did you know that God's children and pearls have a lot in common? Pearls are one of the most precious gems in the whole wide world, and to God, His children are even more precious than pearls!

We can learn a lot about the Christian life by learning about how a pearl is formed. The life of a pearl begins with a gritty grain of sand. Like sin, which entered the world through Adam, an irritating bit of sand enters into an oyster through its shell. Once it gets lodged inside, there's no way for the oyster to get it out. But God...

God gave oysters the gift of nacre, just like He gave us the gift of His Word. The rainbow-sheened nacre is one of the strongest materials in nature. It soothes the oyster while encasing the gritty sand, layer upon layer, until a brilliant, luminous pearl begins to luster and shine. Similarly, God's Word encases our sins, line upon line, precept upon precept, and forms a new creation in us that soon begins to luster and shine!

Miraculously, nacre is made up of millions of crystals. No human effort has ever been able to create such an amazing substance! Each crystal within the nacre lines up perfectly, allowing the light that passes across one crystal to reflect and refract across the other crystals. This lustrous tapestry of light and color is called iridescence.

Nacre, time and consistency increase a pearl's iridescence. In God's children, time and consistency in His Word do the same for them, spiritually. In the world of gems, the greater a pearl's iridescence, the more precious its value. Are you ready to trust Christ with the gritty grains of sin in your heart?

Let's review these vital Bible truths:

According to God, There is none righteous, no, not one (Romans 3:10)
For all have sinned, and come short of the glory of God (Romans 3:23)
...God Commendeth his love toward us, in that, while we were yet sinners, Christ died for us. (Romans 5:8)
For God so loved the world, that he gave his only begotten Son, that whosoever believeth in him should not perish, but have everlasting life. (John 3:16)
For the wages of sin is death; but the gift of God is eternal life through Jesus Christ our Lord. (Romans 6:23)
...If thou shalt confess with thy mouth the Lord Jesus, and shalt believe in thine heart that God hath raised him from the dead, thou shalt be saved. For with the heart man believeth unto righteousness; and with the mouth confession is made unto salvation. (Romans 10:9-10)
For whosoever shall call upon the name of the Lord shall be saved. (Romans 10:13)

If you would like to be born again, just get alone with God and pray something like this:
Dear God, I realize that I am a sinner, and my sin separated me from you. Please forgive me and cleanse me of all unrighteousness. I accept that your Son, Jesus Christ, died to pay for my sins. I believe that He rose again to give me new life in Him forever. I ask you to come live in my heart and become the Lord and Savior of my life. Amen.

If you believed on the Lord Jesus Christ, and prayed a prayer like this one, please let us know at BornTwiceBooks.com! We would love the opportunity to pray for you and send you some special resources to help you grow in your precious walk with God!

ABOUT THE AUTHORS

MUNA & NORA

Nora McElwain and Muna Haddad are cousins whose lives have always seemed to be intertwined by a special spiritual thread.

Being born only a few weeks apart, they are the same age! They share many memories, which formed while they attended the same elementary school. Growing up, Nora was always drawing, painting and writing stories, while Muna was always singing, performing and writing poetry.

Throughout their lives, they confided in one another about their dreams, hopes and goals. Long before they knew they would create books together, however, Nora and Muna each earned their Masters degrees in Education and Theology, respectively. They both became Christian school teachers, wives and mothers as well.

Still, there is one major difference between them: Muna came to know Jesus Christ, as her personal Lord and Savior, at the tender age of 7. Meanwhile, Nora inherited the title "Christian" by birth but did not truly surrender her heart to Christ until she began reading His Word and encountering the Holy Spirit decades later at the age of 30.

By either measure, both Muna and Nora have experienced how powerful the Word of God can be in transforming a life. God says, in Isaiah 55:11, So shall my word be that goeth forth out of my mouth: it shall not return unto me void, but it shall accomplish that which I please, and it shall prosper in the thing whereto I sent it. That is why every song, story, poem or illustration these ladies create together or individually is rooted in the Holy Scriptures.

Visit NoraMcElwain.com to read all about Nora's background, testimony, and books on the horizon—including her upcoming book, The Starfisher. Also, visit MunaHaddad.com for more on Muna's background, testimony, and current projects! Finally, be sure to visit BornTwiceBooks.com to find more God-centered books for the whole family to enjoy!

www.ingramcontent.com/pod-product-compliance
Lightning Source LLC
Chambersburg PA
CBHW042004150426
43194CB00002B/126